There Is Nothing Wrong With Saying So What

There Is Nothing Wrong With Saying So What

An Inspirational, Self-Help Journal

Ella Destiny

Published by Tablo

Table of Contents

This book is dedicated to my father, Ronnie McLendon, Sr., who passed away June 19, 2020, from COVID-19.

Thank you, Dad, for your unwavering love for us. Thank you for the car rides, the conversations, the lessons, the LOVE, and the protection. Thank you for believing in me when I didn't believe in myself—for encouraging me with every thought or idea I brought to you, even if it was "the dumbest mess you ever heard! Thank you for religiously educating me and making sure I always knew to put GOD first—ALWAYS in ALL WAYS!

Thank you, Dad, for the legacy you've left behind!

Acknowledgements

I've always been the type of person to have the craziest faith—to come up with the craziest ideas and just do it! I never really cared about what anybody thought or how they felt, except my dad. Even with him, I'd do it and then tell him—his facial expressions would always say it ALL! But he believed in me, just like my children. I know they probably more times than not thought, Oh gosh, here she go again, but they trusted me enough to know that whatever I did, it was going to be beneficial to us—it wasn't going to hurt us—and they got a chance to see the strength of their mother. No matter what we were "growing" through, no matter what circumstances came our way, no matter how bad or down we were, their mother would always say, "SO WHAT," and they KNEW by the grace of God we'd get through it and come out on top!

First and foremost, I HAVE to thank God who is truly the head of my life. I couldn't begin or end my days without Him. Thank you, God, for always having my back and loving me even in all of my undeserving ways.

My Mister—I'm so thankful to God for sending you to be a part of my life. Your care and concern for my well-being, the way you never hesitate to go above and beyond for not only myself, but for everyone around me as well. Thank you for praying with me, loving me, liking me, holding me accountable and responsible for my actions. Thank you for being all that I need. God knew just what I needed when he allowed me you!

Bria, Donnie, and Little, thank y'all soooooo much for always riding with me NO MATTER WHAT! Thank y'all for encouraging me, pushing me, taking care of me when I was down soooo many times, being obedient and not making it hard for me to parent you all. Thank you for being all I needed you all to be when I needed it. We've been THROUGH SOME

STUFF, but you never judged, never not believed, and never gave up. I LOVE Y'ALL BIG!

My grand-girl Riley! Oh, how I admire your strength. You've endured a LOT in your little four years, but you've also taught me a lot about not being afraid, about unconditional love, and about loving who you are. My Dink—I love you, my girl!

My ladybug, Mommy, you are THE STRONGEST WOMAN I KNOW! I love you to the moon and back! Thank you for being just who you are. You go above and beyond for your children (sometimes too much), and we are so blessed to have you! Your love, care, concern, your willingness to compromise, and your sometimes unsolicited opinions ☺ are all the things that made us who we are. Thank you for showing me what true love, dedication, and strength look like. You KNOW we got you for LIFE, girl!

My SIBS! Good morning, Mo! Awww, man, I'm so thankful to God for my ones! Even though we don't always see eye to eye, we "see" each other, we love each other, we support each other, and we go to war for each other, TOGETHER! I'm so glad God chose this crew for me to do life with. Y'all get on my LAST nerves, but I wouldn't change it for the world! My Yo, all the conversations, the "go ahead, I believe you can do it," the "girl, it don't matter what they say, do what makes you happy . . . if you're happy, I'm happy!" I love and appreciate your loyalty—thank you! My wombmate, my twin, my MoTIP . . . boy, you give me the bluesssssssss! You want to be older than me so bad (give me my whole eight)! Thanks, my guy, for stepping in and up for all of us. Thank you for allowing me to be me even when I get on your nerves! Thank you for letting me "roll with a brother" at times when I just need a break, when I need to feel your energy, or just when I need you! I love you, my dude. God blessed us with an AUTHENTIC ONE with you!

My SAPS! Y'all so ratchet (is that even a word?) in the spirit! Zenneia, Porsha, Sade', Buffie—thank y'all for being my spiritual accountability partners! Thank y'all for NEVER hesitating to stop everything and pray with and for me when I'm going through. Thank y'all for holding me accountable spiritually when I'm not being obedient to God's word, His will, or His way. Thank y'all for not being afraid to show me, ME! You girls are quick to check a sista and don't care how I feel about it—sheesh—but I love and thank y'all for the transparency, for being able to come at me out of a place of love and not judgment or being "messy" (catch the shade). I love y'all lots and appreciate this fivesome!

My spiritual guide, my "Girl, don't call me if it's about so and so," my "I thought you said," my hold me down, go-to, go for, go hard . . . Princess Laya (Laina). THANK YOU!

My fav Bishop Anita O'Brien, ever since I was a little girl watching you in church, I always admired your strength, your dedication, your love, and passion for God. Thank you for sowing into me daily. For your leadership, your guidance, your prayers. Thank you for your input and support with this book. I love and appreciate you!

My GG . . . The Honorable Judge Gladys Weatherspoon! Lady, you have no idea how when I ministered to you during your campaign, I was ministering to myself! I watched your diligence, determination, your strength, and willingness to NOT give up when they told you "no." You kicked butt all the way to the finish line, gracefully! You inspired me to keep going even when there were so many hoping you'd drop out, give up, and not finish the fight. Thank you for always reminding me to "not let anyone overshadow or dim my light." That conversation on your couch that day changed my life forever! I love you so big!

Terrer, Straw, Larreice, Diamond, Pinky, Duck, Q, my aunties and uncles, my best friend Venus, and everyone who's been here with and for me, THANK YOU! I love y'all DOWN, and I thank God for the role each and every one of you play in my life!

Y'all know I'm quick to say, "SO WHAT" and not give a second thought about how anybody feel!

You may think this book is about that, but you'll soon find it's the complete opposite!

Introduction

In the spring of 2020, my dad was getting closer and closer to retirement. He was soooo excited about finally hanging up his work hat, building his house in Hartsville, South Carolina, and taking on his dream retirement job as a Walmart greeter! Don't laugh at my dad—that was his job, and he was sticking to it!

My dad and I, for about three years, carpooled to work every single day. My dad was always one who had a solution for everything we thought was a problem. Working in downtown DC, paying for parking was OUT OF THIS WORLD! I don't care how much money you make—take a job in DC and drive to work, and your gas and parking will guarantee to be more than your paycheck! Me being the "baby girl," and who I think was my dad's favorite (I know my sibs are sick of my mess), I expressed to my dad that $13 a day for parking AND gas is just a bit much for this girl to take, chile! Well, he—being who he was—suggested that if my mom dropped him off in the mornings, I could come get him, and he'd take me to my job and then keep the car and park in their FREE parking lot! Aye, he ain't have to tell me twice. What you say, Dad? Thanks for rolling with a sista!

My dad was always that kind and generous. Everyone else's problem became his, and he'd always, by the grace of God, come up with a solution.

Well, our car rides and car conversations were something else! You'd get an ENTIRE sermon, three-hour conversation, lesson, quiz, and everything else on the ride home. There was not ONE DAY that he didn't have something to say—sometimes too much!

One day, I took him home and decided to go up and sit for a while. I didn't have anything to do, and we were finishing a conversation about him retiring. My dad always walked around with this clipboard; for some reason, he just always had "stuff." Well, this day, he walked in the room talking about his countdown and how he had all of these signs hanging on the walls in his office; he'd always talk about how he'd get on everyone's nerves with the signs, but that he didn't care.

"Hell, I'm retiring in a month" were his words. He came back in the living room with a piece of paper off of that clip board and stood in front of me, cracking up laughing at himself (he always thought his jokes were just the funniest), holding up this sign that said, "There Is Nothing Wrong with Saying So What."

I said, "Dad, they are going to put you out of that place!" His reply—he just held up the sign, and I snapped the picture!

I didn't get it then, but I get it now . . . which brings me to the title of this book.

My dad passed away on June 19, 2020, and as I was going through pictures in my phone, this one in particular popped up and grabbed me. It took me back to that day, but it gave me a different meaning.

As you read this book and take this journey, you'll come to understand why I chose this title, and my hope is that you'll have a different outlook and a changed mind about life, how you approach situations, and how you "grow" through and come out of them.

The Bible has so many stories of every single situation that we are facing, have faced, or will face in our lives, and the Word says, "There's nothing new under the sun." THAT is the TRUTH!

With that being said, THERE IS NOTHING WRONG WITH SAYING SO WHAT!

No I Ain't Got A Job But...So What

One of my favorite lines is from Jazmine Sullivan's song, "Mascara." THAT song is my song! My girl clearly says, "SO WHAT" in a LOT of scenarios and regardless of what's going on in her life; it don't matter as long as she got her makeup on and her mascara in her pocket! Now don't get me wrong—depending on your situation and circumstances, you need a job or some type of means of income, and makeup and mascara ain't gonna get it unless your career field is a makeup artist!

Anyway, the reason I fell in love with this specific line in this song is that it reminded me of those times where I didn't have a job, where I felt like I was inadequate because I couldn't afford to do things or provide for my children the way "the world" says that I should. My self-esteem was pretty low, and the only thing that made me feel like something was when I dressed up and "put my makeup on." Back then, I wasn't really spiritually connected, and so my ways of thinking were all wrong. What I'd come to know in my spiritual growth was that it was okay to say, "SO WHAT" to me not being employed. So now y'all probably think I'm crazy . . . like, this girl is out of her mind saying so what that she don't have a job! Guess what? You're right! I was out of my mind believing it was a job that made me. It was my job that kept me going. It was my job this and my job that—so much that my "job" was taken away from me. Yes, my big guy in the sky grounded the girl! Why, you ask? Probably because I wasn't humbled enough. Probably because I didn't steward well over what was entrusted to me. Probably because I was dependent on "my job" and not "my GOD."

Mark 8:36 reminds us, "For what shall it profit a man, if he shall gain the whole world, but lose his soul?"

That was me . . . you couldn't tell me NOTHING, honey!!! I was at the top

of my game . . . my good paying, "good government job." Ha! Babyyyy, I
HAD IT ALL!

You may be "growing" through a season in your life right now, where
you are in between jobs, your contract just ended, your place of
employment has been "shut down" due to this whole pandemic thing, or
you just can't find work . . . and guess what? "SO WHAT!"

Luke 12:15 says, "Watch out! Be on your guard against all kinds of greed;
life does not consist in abundance of possessions."

More times than not, we are overly consumed with the world and things
thereof. Our worldly thoughts will have us to believe it's "our good job"
that allowed us to buy that car, or that house, or the latest trends of fashion.
I'm sure we've all heard somebody in our lifetime quote the phrase "my
good government job"! The truth is, lots of people rely solely on their
businesses or places of employment as a means of survival, not taking into
account that GOD is our provider. He is the source for our resources, and
if we rely on HIM instead of this world, all of our needs will surely be
met. We don't have to worry about where our next meal is coming from, if
we'll get hired for that next job, how we'll pay our bills, or take care of our
families. If we trust and believe in God, take him at his word, and rest upon
his promises, all of those things will be given to us.

I'm often reminded that sometimes the blessing isn't in what God gives
you, but in what he takes away! I believe—as a matter of fact—I KNOW
his taking away my job at the time he did wasn't to hurt me but to help
me. I needed to be reminded of who HE is and the power in what HE can
do to and for me. I needed to get out of my own way, and what other way
could that happen than by God stripping me of everything that I thought
was important to get my attention. I needed to depend completely on
HIM, to spend more time with my family, to learn patience, humility, and
to strengthen my faith. Whatever being unemployed looked like for me,
I needed it. I had to learn not to look for the good or bad in situations,

but always for God. He has a way of talking to us through people, places, and situations, and sometimes that loss of a job could be God's way of reminding you of who he is or brining something out of you that you didn't even know was there. It could be that he has a better position for you. "God doesn't call the qualified; he qualifies the called." He may not want you to be the janitor because he's qualified you to be the supervisor. He may not even want you to be the supervisor because he's qualified you to be the CEO!

Whatever the situation is, trust God and know that there is a place and purpose just for you!

Bible references for worry, provision, faith, fear, and God's plan:

Isaiah 55:8–9
"'My thoughts are not your thoughts, and my ways are not your ways'" declares the Lord. "'As the heavens are higher than the earth, so are my ways higher than your ways and my thoughts than your thoughts.'"

Psalms 33:11
"The Lord's plan stands firm forever. His thoughts stand firm in every generation."

Philippians 4:19
"And my God will supply all your needs according to His riches in glory in Christ Jesus."

Proverbs 10:3
"The Lord will not let the righteous go hungry, but he denies the wicked what they crave."

The Power of Healing

"Mr. and Mrs. McLendon, we're so sorry to inform you, we had to bag your daughter 3 times...she didn't make it" or whatever they said...

Eleven abdominal surgeries, cysts on my kidney, stitches, staples, drain tubes, no navel, scarred from being cut hip to hip, spending weeks in the hospital fighting for my life, and STILL NO feeling in my abdomen whatsoever due to my nerves having to be cut through, and guess what? SO WHAT!

So now I KNOW y'all think I have completely LOST IT! Not at all. For years, I suffered from endometriosis (all of my sistas know what I'm talking about). Severe cramps, week-long cycles, blood transfusions, days where the only thing I could do to relieve the pain was just lie in the bed crying and rocking, rocking and crying. Ya girl had it BAD! Lots of times, I used to wonder, *Why me?* until I was reminded of the woman in the Bible with the issue of blood, and then I decided, *Why NOT me?*

Matthew 9:20–22 tells the story, "Just then a woman who had been subject to bleeding for twelve years came up behind him and touched the edge of his cloak. She said to herself, 'If I only touch his cloak, I will be healed.'"

Let me tell y'all something. When I say I felt like that was ME bleeding for

12 years . . . OMG! I used to think somebody had it out for me, like that was getting back for something I probably did as a kid or something. Guess what—that may be partially right. Up until maybe a few years ago, I never really liked "sitting in my own truth," especially when someone was calling me to the carpet on MY OWN MESS! In my Tami Roman voice, "Who gon check me, boo?" No really, I used to think that until God sat my butt down, more than TWICE! I was on a path of destruction. I'm not the person I am now—that's for sure.

I had a "don't care" attitude, didn't care who I hurt or pissed off, and whoever got in my way—they "got it" just because. The things and people I should've cared about I didn't, and the people who could give two hoots about me—well, let's just say they got all of my attention.

Every time I stepped all the way outside of myself, God got me ALL THE WAY TOGETHER! Yep, you heard me. I'd get sick, get better, start doing the same exact things, and the next time, my illness would become worse. It wasn't until I really got onto my spiritual path that I started to realize what was happening, and even then, it wasn't enough to stop me. God had to sit me down LITERALLY to get me back in alignment with him.

So, I dare NOT complain about any illness, pain, or suffering that I've gone through. I understand God will chasten us, not because he wants to hurt us, but because he loves us ENOUGH.

"Have you tried my servant Job?" was one of my dad's favorite scriptures in the Bible. In his life lessons to us, he'd always reference this verse when we'd come to him with our issues, and he'd insert our own names: "Have you tried my servant Ella?" It comes from **Job 1:8** when God asks the enemy where he's coming from. He says, "From roaming the earth going back and forth looking for who I could seek, devour and destroy." Then, God poses the question about Job. See, God knew Job's (just like he knows all of our) strength. He KNEW all the enemy would take Job through, but that Job would NEVER curse him.

That's OUR test. Are we strong enough, bold enough, courageous enough? Do we trust God enough that no matter what the enemy brings our way, or what even God ALLOWS to happen, we'd say "so what"? See, God gives allowances and approvals, and just because he "allows" something to happen doesn't necessarily means he "approves" it.

The one thing we should all KNOW is that God is a healer and a deliverer. He is the doctor in a sick room, and by HIS stripes, we are all healed. Whatever illness in your body, your mind, your spirit . . . GOD can bring you through. You may be bedridden or have an incurable illness (how many of us know if God wants to cure it, he can and will?). The doctors may have said there's nothing else they can do. . . . WHOSE REPORT ARE YOU GOING TO BELIEVE?

I'm telling you from experience . . . GOD CAN AND WILL. All you have to do is have faith and believe!

Stories of God healing in the Bible:
God heals Hezekiah's terminal illness: **2 Kings 20:1–11**
Jesus heals the blind man: **John 9:1–2**
Naaman was cured of Leprosy: **2 Kings 5:1–14**
The woman with the issue of blood: **Luke 8:43–48**

Who Are They?

Matthew 12:46–50

While Jesus was still talking to the crowd, his mother and brothers stood outside, wanting to speak to him. Someone told him, "your mother and brothers are standing outside, wanting to speak to you."

He replied to him, "Who is my mother and who are my brothers?" Pointing to his disciples, he said, "Here are my mother and my brothers. For whoever does the will of my Father in heaven is my brother and sister and mother."

Awwww . . . so you got into a fight with a friend or family member, maybe a co-worker, and now you aren't speaking anymore . . . SO WHAT!

How many times have you been in a situation or even been around someone who stopped talking to you . . . a close friend, family member, or co-worker? It happens every single day, and lots of times, people will say, "It's petty," "It doesn't make any sense," "That's his or her sister or brother," "If that were me . . ."

Let me tell you something. I have people in my own family who will sit at a table, break bread with me, and the second I walk away, talk A WHOLE LOTTA stuff behind my back—and guess what . . . SO WHAT!

I've come to learn on this journey that more and more often, you HAVE to let go of those around you that are NOT of God and NOT doing the will of God. It doesn't mean that they're bad people, that you think you're better than they are, or that you have your stuff all together. It just means that you are in a different place and space in your life, on your path and on your journey, and some people just don't fit or don't align with the plan God has for YOU.

What does that mean? It means there will be people around you at work, in your immediate family, even in your own household whose beliefs, morals, and values are the complete opposite of you and yours, and just because they are your mother, your father, your children, neighbors, or co-workers, you're supposed to cut your eyes to the intentional sin they commit. Don't get me wrong—we all "sin and fall short of the glory of God." However, when it's INTENTIONAL, like they know they're committing a sin . . . you better hit feet fast (runnnnnnnnn)!

Here's why. **1 Corinthians 15:33** says, "Do not be misled: bad company corrupts good character." THAT MEANS beloved, if your circle isn't tight, if the people you surround yourself with—NO MATTER WHO IT IS—ain't living right, guess what? Nine times out of ten, YOU won't be either! Oh, you think because Jo-Jo was the one that robbed the bank and you were "just" with him, you won't go down for it too? What planet are YOU living on? More than likely, EVEN if you just drove the car to take your "homie" to the bank and he didn't tell you he was actually going to rob it, you, my friend, are just as guilty as he is. The same with God . . . if you KNOWINGLY allow your sister, brother, mother, father, or cousin to sin, you're in the midst of it. If you don't "spiritually check them" or REMOVE yourself, God will CHASTISE YOU TOO, and it won't matter what "they" say about you cutting your folks off!

Listen, **Matthew 5:30** tells us that "if your right hand causes you to steal, cut it off and throw it away. It is better for you to lose one part of your body than for your whole body to go to hell."

Soooooo . . . what does that mean? It means I DON'T GIVE A CARE WHO DON'T LIKE IT . . . SOOOOOO WHAT! If it or they or them mean me NO GOOD and they're going to cause me to get in trouble with MY GOD, I'm cutting you off, NO IFS, ANDS, OR BUTS about it!

Y'all, if Jesus cut off his MOTHER AND BROTHERS, PLEASE believe y'all don't stand a chance . . . IJS (I'm just saying)!

Proverbs 13:20 tells us to "walk with the wise and become wise, for a companion of fools suffers harm."

Don't get all in your feelings because you have to cut somebody off or if they even stop talking to you. Know that God is the end all, and he will reveal to you what's best for you willingly or forcefully.

You ever been in a situation where you knew you weren't supposed to be dealing with, or no longer be friends with a certain person, but you just can't find the nerve to tell that person or bring yourself to cut them off, and then all of a sudden, they pick a fight with you, break up with you, or tell you "they just can't do you anymore"? Ohhhh, BUT GOD . . . they say he has a sense of humor, right? See . . . all you have to do is pray about it, sit back, and TRUST GOD! HE will ALWAYS show up!

What About You?

Sooooo . . . now that I've told you a little about me, tell YOU a little about YOU! Sounds funny, right? I know, you're thinking, *What in the world does she mean?*

What I mean is, sometimes we are so distracted and caught up in this world until everything is a problem. We allow things that shouldn't really matter to matter, and we forget about what's important.

When we'd have conversations with my dad, he'd often ask, "Has man forgotten GOD?"

Well, this is your opportunity to reflect on things or situations that should have been your "SO WHAT" moment, but instead, you tried to be self-sufficient, thinking you can fix people, places, or things all on your own, forgetting that there's a spirit, the True and Living GOD, that can and will meet your needs and supply them according to HIS riches in glory.

Take this moment now to SIT IN YOUR TRUTH, FACE IT, FIX IT, AND SAY, "SO WHAT!"

1. There was a time in my life where instead of saying, "so what,"
I_____

_____.

I didn't know then _____ , but now

I_____,
and I can turn it over to God and say, "So what!"

2. Dear _____, *you ARE stronger than you think! God*

has already worked out _____ , and you
no longer have to worry about it. He has gone forward on your behalf
and _____ . When you think about
where you've come from and other people in worse situations than you,
you can now look at yourself and say, "So what!" You can thank God
for   allowing   you   to   "grow"   through
_____
because you've found the GOD in it, and you know that it was for your
GOOD!

1 John 1:9 teaches us, "If we confess our sins, he is faithful and just to
forgive us our sins, and to cleanse us from all unrighteousness."

Whatever sins you may have committed knowingly and unknowingly,
confess them to God first, ask for forgiveness, and then forgive yourself. We
ALL have some "stuff" we have to own, face, and fix, but we can't heal or
get better if we don't let it out and fix it first! Talk to yourself in the shower,
girl, (y'all know we do that sometimes anyway)! Whatever you have to do
to get back to your TRUE self, DO IT! Don't be ashamed of your faults,
flaws, and mistakes. It's when we DON'T fix them that it's a problem. So,
when you get in your bag and start feeling some type of way, PRAY, and
then say, "SO WHAT!"

S.A.P.s (Spiritual Accountability Partners)

So, the conversation went something like this: *phone rings*

me: Hey girl . . . OMG! I need ***screechhhhhhhhh***

her: Ummmmm . . . I KNOW you're not calling me asking me for NOTHING!
(I may be being a little extra, but it was the tone for me!) I don't want to
pray for you. I know it's not right and it's not God, but let me tell you about
YOU! I've been texting you to check on you because I was worried, and you
never responded. I know you're going through something right now, but so am
I, and it's NOT ABOUT YOU! People reach out to you to show their love and
concern, and you completely ignore them. You "shut down" or disappear until
YOU deal with whatever it is you're going through and then expect the world
to be ready and waiting when you decide to come back. You do it all the time,
and it's not fair to everyone else.

THAT was a conversation I had with one of my SAPs (SPIRITUAL
ACCOUNTABILITY PARTNERS). Sis DUG IN MY MESS that day and was
NOT here for the shenanigans! At first, I was like, "Who in the heck does
she think she talking to?" But then, the spiritual me was like, "You're right,
and I am so sorry!" Now, if you don't have somebody like THAT in your
life, YOU NEED TO SWITCH YOUR CIRCLE!

I used to think that the world revolved around me—and my dad often
said to me growing up that the world didn't revolve around me... ARE
YOU SURE? I AM WHO I AM, AND IT DOES! I had people around me
who were afraid to tell me "no" or "that's not right," and let me tell y'all,
that stuff MESSED. ME. UP!

I didn't have an ounce of empathy or sympathy for NOBODY . . . for what? It was all about Ella . . . what Ella wanted, she got. And I had the meanest attitude if I didn't, to the point where folks would justify my toxic behavior by saying, "You know how she is" or "Please don't get her started." THAT was soooo UGLY! I was the worst!

I'm so glad that's not me anymore, and I'm so thankful to GOD for placing people in my life to "check me spiritually" and get me together. People who love me enough to say, "I'm not here to cater to your attitude or feelings; I'm here to love on you, support you, encourage you, but also tell you when your butt is wrong!" We ALL need us some SAPs in our lives.

If you don't have none, GET SOME! It's so worth it to have someone to show you, YOU! It's not always easy, and almost always, it's uncomfortable, but growth and comfort don't mix. If you want to grow in your "spiritual" being, you're going to have to be in uncomfortable situations, have uncomfortable conversations, and maybe even go to uncomfortable places. That's where the real growth takes place!

1 Corinthians 13:11: "When I was a child, I talked like a child, I thought like a child, I reasoned like a child. When I became a man, I put the ways of childhood behind me."

"SO WHAT"—you have someone in your life that's willing to take the time to call you to the carpet on your mess! It's not because they just want to pick on you or are always so ready to talk about all the bad you've done or continue to do. It's because like God, they love you in spite of YOU. They love you ENOUGH, and you'd better thank God for that person or people that will sit with you in your situations, love you past your faults, and stand with you when you're RIGHT! Someone that will hold you accountable for your mess because they want to see you do better and grow into the person that GOD has called you to be—and NOT participate in your pity parties.

Thank you, GOD, for my SAPS! Thank you that we are all and can be transparent with one another, checking each other spiritually from a place of love and not malice or hurt. Thank you that we love each other enough to speak the truth even when it's not what we WANT to hear but what we NEED to hear. Thank you that we are all in communion with you, and that we all know how to call on you when ourselves or each other are in need. Thank you, God, for the assignment that we have on each other's lives and your intentionality in placing us there. God, please always allow us to love and respect one another in the hardest of times, and when it's all we can do . . . I ask these things in your name. Selah.

S.A.P. Check

WHO'S IN YOUR CIRCLE?

Here is a quick checklist to evaluate who's in your circle. Who are the people that you're in communion with on a daily basis? Are they SAPs or just people that you're around? How are they depositing into your mental, physical, and spiritual growth?

- Prayer partner
- Accountability partner
- Someone who tells you when you're wrong
- Workout partner
- Someone who allows you to vent without passing judgment
- Someone who won't let you sit in situations too long
- Someone who tells you to "get up" when you're feeling down
- Someone who is protecting your peace
- Someone who won't come telling you what "they" said because they know where you're trying to go and they don't want to poison your spirit
- Someone who isn't afraid to tell you "SO WHAT"

My dad used to always say, "In order to be or have friends, you must present yourself friendly," and while you can't change the people around you, you can change the people around you (catch that and read it again)!

Take a moment to reflect on the people closest to you; if they aren't depositing into your spiritual being . . . well, think about whether you should let them stick around or not. Don't be afraid to let go of what is not serving a spiritual purpose in your life.

Proverbs 13:20

"He that walketh with wise men shall be wise, but a companion of fools shall be destroyed."

Single Momma Drama

OH NO! Your husband, boyfriend, baby daddy left you to raise these kids all by yourself . . . "SO WHAT!"

You ever read the story of Hagar in the Bible? It's in the book of Genesis. If you haven't read it, SHAME ON YOU! Oh yes, we're not the only ones who had baby daddies who gave us these kids and then left, and to be honest, Hagar's story may be a little worse.

Genesis 21:14 reminds us that Abraham (Abram), after getting this girl pregnant WITH PERMISSION TO SLEEP WITH HER FROM HIS WIFE, gives this child bread and a bottle of water and tells her to "take off skipping" with THEIR SON!

NOW . . . truth of the matter is, Hagar was the "slave handmaiden" of Sarai and could have only gotten pregnant because her mistress insisted. The ancient practice was if the wife couldn't provide a child herself, she could give her handmaiden to her husband and if she conceived, that child would be attributed as the wife's child.

The law of Mesopotamia that Abram and Sarai derived from was if you sent a servant or slave away, the owner was only required to provide them bread and water. Ishmael was not the son of promise but "the son of Sarai's will." Because she wasn't willing to wait for God's promise, she foolishly pushed her agenda. When we read the Biblical text, we see that Abram didn't want to send them away. He had spent at least 13 years raising Ishmael; HOWEVER, the fact still remains that Hagar was in "single mother" position and crisis. Yet, because God promised to bless "all" of Abram's seed, the promise was conferred on Ishmael (her son), as well.

Reminds me of MY story! I didn't give permission, but my then husband, after us having three children and being married for about eight years, got somebody else pregnant and pretty much told me to kick rocks with my babies! Yep, happened to me too, and that's why I can say, "SO WHAT!"

When I was raising my children as a single mother, especially my daughter, I always stressed to them and reminded myself that whether the father was there or not, I HAD TO! I couldn't check out, I couldn't call out sick, I couldn't take a break . . . I HAD to be there for them, and believe me, we went through SOME STUFF! There were times when we struggled, times when I had to make the decision to turn over my plate so that my children could eat. Oh yeah, it wasn't all flowers and roses on this side. You may be thinking, *You had your family, your parents—y'all are so close; you didn't have to go through that,* but the truth is, I DID.

Depending on my parents wasn't an option for me. I needed to go through all that I did so that I could mature and grow in my faith! This was my season of having my one-on-one with God and depending SOLELY on him. It was no other way but God's way, and in those times and even now, there was NO MAN that could save me.

Yes, it was hard, yes there were times when I had to go back home and re-group, dust myself off, and try again, but I did it, and by the grace of God, I MADE IT!

Yes, the Word says that man was not made to live alone, and I almost hate it when a woman says, "I don't need a man" because that's not the truth and that's not God. What I will say is, you don't need "the wrong man." Remember when I said God will give us allowances and approvals? Just because he allowed us a "good man" doesn't mean he approved of him!

We always call ourselves "praying for a good man," but do we really know what we're praying for? Lots of times, we don't put specifics on our prayers, and God allows us exactly what we ask for. He may be a "good man" (good looking) but knocks us upside our heads, or always "about to start a business" or "I'm trynna do . . ."—flip this and flip that. You leave for work—he's on the couch and in the same spot when you get back if he ain't dropping you off in YOUR car (Jody looking self)! Yeah sis, be careful what you ask for, and make sure you are specific in those prayers. Ask God for EXACTLY what you want; don't be half stepping, or you gonna get "half" a man!

But seriously, don't be tripping because your man or woman left you, even if you have children. The rest of the story of Hagar goes like this . . . even though Abraham impregnated Hagar and then sent her on her merry little way with their son, she found her faith and her strength and trusted God NO MATTER WHAT! Even though she felt the pain of what happened to her, she continued to raise her son, and God was with her. So much so that God told her in **Genesis 21:18**, "Arise, lift the boy up and take him by the hand, for I will make him into a great nation."

You see THAT! God made that boy GREAT! I'm telling you, there's ALWAYS a PURPOSE for YOUR PAIN!

I went through hell on wheels being a single mother, but it was ALL WORTH IT! My daughter graduated COLLEGE with her degree in Applied Sciences working in her medical career field with the federal government. My oldest SON (that's right, I'm a single mother who raised not one, but TWO African American young men), graduated college CUM LAUDE with his degree in Management and eBusiness and is now in school for his MASTER'S. My youngest son is in his junior year of college getting his degree in Computational Biology (what the heck?)!

I'll say again: SO WHAT he or she left you! Sometimes the blessing isn't in what God gives you—it's in what he takes away!

Keep the Faith

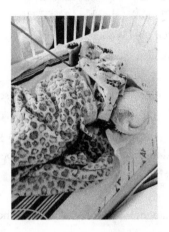

Matthew 17:15: "Lord have mercy on my son," he said. "He has seizures and is suffering greatly. He often falls into the fire or into the water."

June 12, 2017. I remember the day like it was yesterday. I was sitting at my desk at work and got a frantic phone call from my daughter. I couldn't really make out what she was saying because she was crying and screaming. After I told her to calm down so I could hear what she was saying, the words, "Riley is having a seizure" stung my ears like a jelly fish in water. "WHAT! I'M ON MY WAY" was all I could say.

I get to the hospital's emergency room, and everyone is a nervous wreck! To see my one-year-old granddaughter sitting in that bed was something I could've never imagined. It happened though, and my only question was, "God, why?" Now, you know I KNOW BETTER, but we're human, right? And when things like this happen, it's the first thing we wonder.

The doctor comes in and says, "Oh, it's something that happens in children this size a lot; it's nothing serious, and it'll NEVER happen again. Take her home, monitor her, and she'll be just fine."

The VERY NEXT DAY, she has ANOTHER seizure. Back at the hospital, now they tell us, "We need to keep her overnight to run some tests and see what's really going on." You think?

Long story short, after MRIs with sedation, CT scans, and X-rays, they say, "We hate to tell you—Riley has epilepsy." You're kidding, right? My little grand girl who's only been on this earth for a year and two months has epilepsy? What does that even mean? What does that look like? Will she have it the rest of her life? What now?

I watched as my daughter and Riley's dad sat in the windowsill, looking out with the most fear and confusion any young parent could have. Then, I had to get myself together, pray, and remind them of who GOD is, and THAT was my "SO WHAT" moment.

God gives us situations and circumstances to test our faith and strength in HIM! It doesn't mean that you're a bad parent, or that you're necessarily being punished for something, although sometimes God will allow his wrath to come upon our children and our children's children if we aren't obedient to HIS word, HIS will, and HIS way. It could very well mean too that God wants to use YOUR situation to help someone else.

My daughter was enrolled in college at South Carolina State University. Home on her summer break, her pregnancy came as a complete surprise but was more than welcome. I often reminded her throughout the pregnancy to trust God, never feel bad about it, and know she's not the first teen mom and won't be the last. My dad always used to say, "The way you go into these phases will determine how you come out."

When we learned of Riley's illness, it reminded me that God will use ordinary people to do extraordinary things, and I KNEW THIS was one of them! I knew that he was going to show young mothers "SO WHAT," you had a baby at an early age or while you're still in school. You can STILL graduate, go to college, and become successful! "SO WHAT," you have a child with special needs . . . GOD anointed and appointed YOU to parent and care for that child because he knew he'd equip you with all the tools you'll need! He also knew this would teach you lessons, stretch your patience, and grow you in ways you would've never imagined.

Matthew 17:20 goes on to say, "Because you have so little faith. Truly I tell you, if you have faith as small as a mustard seed, you can say to this mountain, 'Move from here to there,' and it will move. Nothing will be impossible for you."

NO MATTER WHAT IT LOOKS LIKE, always keep the faith and know that God has a plan for your life beyond anything you can comprehend.

We KEPT the faith and prayed and prayed for my grand girl to be DELIVERED, and here we are three years later, and my girl is SEIZURE FREE! I SEE YOU, BIG GOD!

Faith Check

How big is your faith? You ever wanted God to do something or move something or show you something in your life, but you didn't have enough faith to believe it would happen? Then, you see later that if you had just held on and believed . . .

Write down three things you should've had faith for but didn't.

1.)

2.)

3.)

Now, write down the steps you need to take to increase your faith, and believe God for the promises of Abraham!

Hebrews 11:1: "Now faith is the assurance of things hoped for, the conviction of things not seen."

Everybody's Looking At Me Like I'm Crazy, and I Am Maybe...

Before Pastor Mike came out with the series about "crazy faith," I was already one to believe and STAND ON THAT . . . my CRAZYYYYY faith! My faith was so big that a lot of times, people thought something was wrong with me! I mean, I'd say something KNOWING THEY thought it was impossible, but I knew MY GOD would make the impossible possible! How many of y'all know God can make the impossible possible (*my good church voice*)?

Do y'all remember when the Wii game console came out? EVERYBODY had one! At one point, it was the thing to do on a Friday night! I'd like to think for a brief time, it brought families back together, spending time and just being able to be a kid again for a little while.

Our family always had Wii parties, especially in the wintertime when it was cold, and you really didn't feel like going out.

I remember this one weekend, we had family over, cooked food, and had the bowling tournament on the Wii. There had to be at least 20 people or more over on a Friday night. I didn't have a job, no money, and no place to go, so that was my entertainment!

That night, my spirit told me to move. Not move like dance or play the game, move like out of my apartment. Mind you, everybody was playing the game, having a good time, eating, and drinking (I don't drink), but everyone was just enjoying their night.

I walked straight in the middle of everybody, turned the game down, and said, "Y'all sitting here acting like we're not moving Wednesday!" If y'all could've seen the expressions on their faces!

I believe my daughter asked me, "Ma, did you take your medicine today?" Remember when I told y'all I had a million surgeries? Well, yes, ya girl was seeing a shrink and taking meds! Yeah, y'all might say that's not what "we" do or you'd never . . . go through half the stuff I've been through, and then let's have a conversation!

Anywho . . . my girl, like everybody else in the house, really thought I was crazy. Like, what in the heck are you talking about? First of all, we NEVER had a conversation about moving NOWHERE. I didn't have a job, and I dang on sure didn't have no money, so what in the world? Guess what? "SO WHAT!"

God showed me and told me, and I believed it, so I was crazy enough to step out there on faith and do just what he said to do!

Fast forward, Sunday comes . . . we go to church, I come home, and open up the *Washington Post*. I go to the employment section, see this personnel security job, and apply for it. (Note, the day is SUNDAY.) I go online and complete the application; not even an hour later, I get a phone call.

The caller says, "I see you've just completed your application online and submitted your resume. I was wondering if you'd be available to come in for an interview TOMORROW!"

Monday comes, I go for the interview, and guess what—HIRED ON THE SPOT! The manager asks if I could start TUESDAY! OHHHHH, BUT I'M NOT DONE YET! REMEMBER I TOLD MY KIDS WE WERE MOVING WEDNESDAY?

Well, I get home from my interview and open up the *Post* yet again. I go to the rentals section and find this really nice townhome. I call the number, and the owner asks if I want to come see the place. Never telling him my situation, I agree. I go see the place and instantly fall in love! The owner and I talk, and I tell him I just got hired for a new job so all I have is an offer letter, no pay stubs, and I don't even have the money to pay a security deposit or first month's rent. OH, BUT GOD! GUESS WHAT? I GOT MY KEYS ON WEDNESDAY! Not ONLY did he accept my offer letter, but he waived my security deposit AND told me when I got my first pay, I could pay HALF of the rent and just catch up on the rest when I could! COME ON, GODDDDD!

I'M TELLING Y'ALL . . . SO WHAT you don't have a job or money or whatever it is you THINK you need—GOD is the SOURCE FOR YOUR RESOURCES, AND ALL YOU HAVE TO DO IS HAVE THE FAITH. HE CAN TURN ANY situation around in YOUR favor! HA HA, yessss, GOD!

There was a time, because I had so many surgeries and was in and out of work for a while, that I was about to be evicted from my apartment. I remember my dad and sister coming over late one night (my eviction was scheduled for the next day) to help get out whatever little things I could carry that was of value. I hadn't even told my children that we were getting put out the next day. I guess you'd say that's messed up, but the way my FAITH is set up, GOD told me, "Don't move."

My dad comes and says, "Did you tell these kids yet? You need to tell them, and we need to get started getting your things out of here."

I'm just sitting on the bed looking at him like HE'S the one that's crazy, and I tell him, "Dad, God told me don't move." He looked at me puzzled, like *girl, you tripping*, and walked out of the room, proceeding to tell my kids what he THOUGHT was about to happen!

Well . . . BY THE GRACE OF GOD, BEFORE my dad and sister left my house THAT NIGHT, MY RENT WAS PAID IN FULL! I'm just here to tell y'all: "SOOOOOOO WHATTTTT!"

Do y'all know where I'm going with this now? I'm just saying . . . WRITE THE VISION, MAKE IT A PLAN, MAKE YOUR REQUEST KNOWN TO GOD. SO WHAT you don't have it or can't see it RIGHT NOW. SPEAK THINGS AS THOUGH THEY WERE!

Friends...how many of us have them?
Friends...the ones you can depend on

What kind of friends do you have? Do they have enough faith for the both of you?

You ever hear the story of the people in Capernaum, where the dudes have a friend that's paralyzed, and they need to get him to Jesus, but it was soooo crowded they couldn't get in the door?

It was four friends, right, and their friend was paralyzed, but they had the faith that if they could just get him in front of Jesus, he'd be healed. Well, there was so many people there, they couldn't get their boy nowhere near the door, soooo they were like, "We just gon tear the roof off this mother!" No really, they took the roof off and lowered their friend down on the mat he was lying on and got him in front of "the man"! Jesus saw how much faith they all had, that he was like, "Your sins are forgiven," and he healed their friend! Look it up in **Mark 2:1–5.**

Listennnnnnnnn . . . THOSE the kind of friends you need on your team!

I had a friend in a situation once. Life happened, she lost a loved one, and was put in a position where her job was in jeopardy. She went back and forth to court, and pretty much, the lawyer said, "If it goes left and the judge says this, you lose your license for five years and pretty much your job." I watched her tirelessly trying to figure out what she'd do, what was going to happen to her livelihood, and all the what-ifs. We went back and forth to court, and finally it came. The judge said the words that none of us wanted to hear, and just like that, her life was turned upside down. My spirit told me THAT wasn't it. My faith for her was sooooo BIG—I just believed God would show up.

I told my friend, "Call your job." Upset and just in total disbelief that she'd for sure lost her job and couldn't reinstate her license for five YEARS, she wasn't trying to hear NOTHING I was saying, and honestly, if I were her in that moment, I probably would've felt the same way. Again, I said, "Call your job." I told her, "I KNOW what the lawyer said, and I was sitting right there to hear what the judge said, but I also know what GOD said, and that's NOT IT; CALL YOUR JOB!"

Hesitant and still upset, she said she'd call. CAN I TELL Y'ALL THE POWER OF GOD? I let my friend out the car and headed home. Before I could even get down the road, my friend called me, giving GOD ALL THE PRAISES! I asked, "You called your job? What happened?" My friend proceeded to tell me that she called her job, and BY THE GRACE OF GOD, THEY TOLD HER, "WE'VE CHANGED THE RULES, AND YOURS IS THE FIRST CASE. COME GET YOUR UNIFORM BACK!" BABYYYYYYYY . . .

"SO WHAT" you may not be in a place where your faith is strong or you're still a babe in believing. All you have to do is surround yourself with the RIGHT PEOPLE, people who will have faith FOR YOU, and God WILL COME THROUGH just like he did for those four friends who carried their paralytic friend! I'm not telling y'all nothing I don't KNOW!

Truth Check

Sometimes in life, it's hard for us to face our truth. When someone who truly loves and cares about us is calling us to the carpet on our stuff, it's uncomfortable. Why? Because for so long, we've been conformed to the ways of this world, and so for us to step out of the box and learn something different, it hurts our feelings. "You didn't have to talk to me like that," or we just don't want to hear it. Where does God get the glory in that?

MY TRUTH is, I've spent or wasted so many years being what this world said I should be, talking the way the world wants me to talk, doing things the world wants me to do, that I didn't realize how messed up I really was. It took for someone who experienced some of the same things I did in life to hold the mirror up to me and show me, ME. THAT was a tough, ugly pill to swallow, but it's MY truth. The "truth" is, you can't make wrong right, and James 5:16 says that we must confess our sins ("truths") one to another and pray for one another that we may be healed.

WHAT ARE SOME AREAS IN YOUR LIFE WHERE YOU ARE NOT BEING TRUTHFUL WITH YOURSELF?

1.)

2.)

3.)

2 Timothy 2:15: "Do your best to present yourself to God as one approved, a worker who does not need to be ashamed and who correctly handles the word of truth."

So If I'm Looking Up Don't Mind Me, But I can't be, I just can't be, I CAN'T be down no more

When my dad passed, it was a MAJOR blow to our family. We were stuck, distraught, lost, in disbelief. We never imagined it being our husband, father, grandfather, brother, cousin, friend. We felt like that was the end-all. I know for myself, I sat with the "now what" for a long time, almost to the point of depression. What do I do now that there are no more phone calls saying, "All right, don't forget about me!" or the "Hey, baby girl"—what he always called me? More than that, what do I do with this pain? What does living without my dad anymore even look like? Losing him was a shock to the heart, and I honestly didn't believe I could take or handle anything else; two months later, my NIL (Niece-in-Love) passed away.

At this point, I'm just like, "God, what is it? What am I supposed to be learning? What am I supposed to be teaching? What am I supposed to be doing? This season is hard God, but I trust you." Now, we'd already lost five close family members, and it was quite clear to me that God was trying to get our attention. It was either poop or get off the pot like my dad would say, and I had to make a decision to waddle in grief and misery or do like **Proverbs 31:17** says and gird myself with strength and show that my arms are strong." I had to GIRD UP THEM LOINS, honey, and get ready for battle!

What I now understood is that while God was busy filling his kingdom, the enemy was even busier looking for who he could devour and destroy, and he knew these were the times that I was at my weakest . . . BUT GOD! From that moment on, I decided NO MATTER WHAT came my way, I would again not look for the good or the bad, but the GOD and continue to "look up" to the hills from whence comes my help. Or, in hip hop terms from my girl Jazmine Sullivan, "So if I'm looking up, don't mind me, but I can't be down no more, and if you don't know where to find me, I'm out looking for the silver lining!"

I started looking for the blessings in the lessons . . . the silver lining!

What the Enemy Can't Destroy He Distracts

Matthew 8 reports numerous healing miracles of Jesus: the man with leprosy, the Centurion's servant, Peter's mother-in-law, and many others. It also reports Jesus' warning of the cost of being his follower, his calming of a storm on the lake of Galilee, and his exorcism of two demon-possessed men.

You ever heard the saying, or better yet the Bible verse, "As for me and my house, we will serve the Lord"? It's there, in **Joshua 24:15.**

It's something our family has always stood on, and my household is no different. I've always taught my children to pray and trust God ALWAYS in ALL WAYS, which is why the enemy used distractions to try to destroy what God had already ordained through my children. I used the example of Matthew 8 to remind you of the complete healing and restoration that God can do if we just follow him.

While I won't share the complete story because it's not mine to tell, I will say that the enemy TRIED IT with my oldest son! Yesssss, indeed . . . my son who graduated college Cum Laude with a degree in Management and eBusiness. My son who's now working on his master's degree in which he'll receive in the summer of 2021. My oldest, DON! I referred to Matthew 8 because the story of the two demon-possessed men was him. What happened to my son was something I would've never imagined. All I can say is that a completely different spirit had taken control of him, his movements, his thoughts, the words that came out of his mouth . . . that was NOT my son! But, just like with those two men, we called on the name of GOD, and with a word, he was healed—after about a week of going through these demonic episodes, fasting, and prayer, by HIS stripes. I'm telling you the power of faith and prayer!

The enemy didn't stop there, though, and at this point, I'm laughing in his face! He came for my daughter not even two weeks after my son was healed. Again, this isn't my story to tell, but boy oh boy! The only thing I could think was, *Is THAT all you got? We've been gut punched this entire year, and by the grace of God, we're STILL standing. What in the world makes you think you'll have us now? NOT NOW, NOT EVER!* The enemy has NO PLACE in our household. You can have all of your antics and tactics and distractions . . . we ain't buying what you trying to sell!

We had minor distractions but we were NOT destroyed!

Matthew 16:23: "Get thee behind me Satan"!

Outro

You may be thinking, *How in the world was she able to write a book with so much going on in her life AND in the middle of a pandemic?!* Truth is, LOTS of times, I don't even know myself. What I do know is, with all the things I've grown through over the years, God has NEVER failed me, and if he's brought me through before, he would most certainly do it again. Losing faith was NEVER an option and should never be for you!

God promises us in his word that he will never leave us or forsake us, and that we can take him at his word and rest upon his promises. Isn't that good news?! That no matter where we've been, what we're going through, God is still here for us, EVEN in our undeserving ways. Yes, we have hard times, uncomfortable moments, times when we don't know what the heck just happened, but we also have a BIG GOD! One that's bigger than all of our hurt, all of our pain, all of our problems, and issues. All he wants is for us to draw nearer to him!

In this guide, we've learned about God's healing, his faithfulness, obedience, miracles, blessings, growth, and maturity, who and where we receive counsel, accountability, grief, and how to move forward in the face of opposition. We've also learned that God is there sitting with us in our situations in the midst of it all.

If you take away nothing else, I want you to always remember, for every obstacle you face in life, there is nothing new under the sun, there's always a purpose for your pain, and THERE IS NOTHING WRONG WITH SAYING SO WHAT!

Please be good to yourselves and each other!
–Ella Destiny

Inspirational Quotes and Affirmations

- Faith isn't about feelings.
- Waiting is time re-purposed.
- Things change when you change things.
- Elevation takes separation.
- You can't change the people around you, but you can change the people around you.
- If it's hard, it's worth it . . . nothing good comes easy.
- Stop expecting YOU from people.
- Every miracle in the Bible first started as a problem.
- Speak LIFE.
- Trust God as your SOURCE to provide your RESOURCES.
- I am NOT defeated.
- I am HEALED.
- I have no worries or frustrations.
- I am not lonely.
- I am content.

In Memory of:

#LLAuntTook #LLAuntie #LLBritt #LLNeicey
#LLVett #LLUncleBlue #LLUncleRonnie

1 Corinthians 15:55: "*O death, where is thy sting? O grave, where is thy victory?*"

I think we can all attest to the fact that the year of 2020 has been the most trying! Loss after loss, death after death. Mental loss, loss of jobs, relationships, faith . . . death of loved ones, family members, friends—even death of our own wellbeing, meaning we started to neglect our mental, physical and spiritual health. **Psalms 107:13–14** says, "Then they cried to the Lord in their trouble, and he delivered them from their distress. He brought them out of darkness and the shadow of death and burst their bonds apart." The good news is, regardless of what binds us, physical illness, mental struggles, death, whatever the situation may be, God will free us from all our pain.

The question is, "So what now?" What do you do with all the loss you've endured, the pain you've experienced, the feelings of uncertainty? GIVE IT TO GOD!

Matthew 5:4: "Blessed are they that mourn, for they shall be comforted." God's strength always works best in our weakness. We may be at or have been at some of our weakest moments, but don't EVER give up on God because he will NEVER give up on you. He has promised us the blessings of Abraham, and that is one word that we can stand on.

Rest in peace to all of those we've lost this year . . . may your memories live on in and through us!

Yvette Aaron
Willie Mae Aaron
Brittany Powell
Selena Addison
Shirley Green
NaTonya Murphy
Ernest Addison
Pastor Sylvester Thompson
Felicia Jones
Alice Mack
Ronnie McLendon, Sr.

About the Author

Entrepreneur, Author, Mom , Motivational Speaker

Mother, Grandmother, Daughter, Sister, Cousin, Friend . . . Ella Destiny is a survivor of all things LIFE! From 11 abdominal surgeries to doctors saying she didn't make it to the loss of her father, Ella has a testimony of the greatness of God. Whether she is speaking to a crowd or in an intimate conversation, you're sure to get a "Come on, God" in mid-conversation because she is always ready to revere the Almighty with a song in her heart and a praise on her lips! Through ups and downs, good and bad, trials and tribulations, the things she has always been able to stand on are the word of God, her faith, and her strength knowing "from whence comes" her help. We are all told, "Live your life to the fullest." She is here to do just that. Ella Destiny serves as a vessel to project her passions, clue her loyal tribe as to what inspires her in this crazy world, and live ON PURPOSE!

LONG LIVE MY DAD

In Loving Memory of Mr. Ronnie
McLendon, Sr.

CPSIA information can be obtained
at www.ICGtesting.com
Printed in the USA
BVHW031417250321
603272BV00011B/1139